T0365865

Jesus
LOVES ME

RICHARD A. RAINWATER
Illustrations by Windel Eborlas

Order this book online at www.trafford.com
or email orders@trafford.com

Most Trafford titles are also available at major online book retailers.

Printed in the United States of America.

ISBN: 978-1-4907-4141-3 (sc)
ISBN: 978-1-4907-4142-0 (e)

Library of Congress Control Number: 2014912115

Our mission is to efficiently provide the world's finest, most comprehensive book publishing service, enabling every author to experience
success. To find out how to publish your book, your way, and have it available worldwide, visit us online at www.trafford.com

Trafford rev. 07/08/2014

 www.trafford.com

North America & international
toll-free: 1 888 232 4444 (USA & Canada)
fax: 812 355 4082

It was a very nice morning. There was not a cloud in the sky. William was outside playing with his dog. He loved playing with his dog, his best friend.

People were walking up and down the street without a worry in the world. They were shopping and talking with each other. Everything was perfect.

Suddenly, a man came running down the street. Throughout the town, he was yelling, "He's coming! He's coming!"

William thought to himself, *Who's coming? It must be someone real important. I better go tell Mom and Dad.*

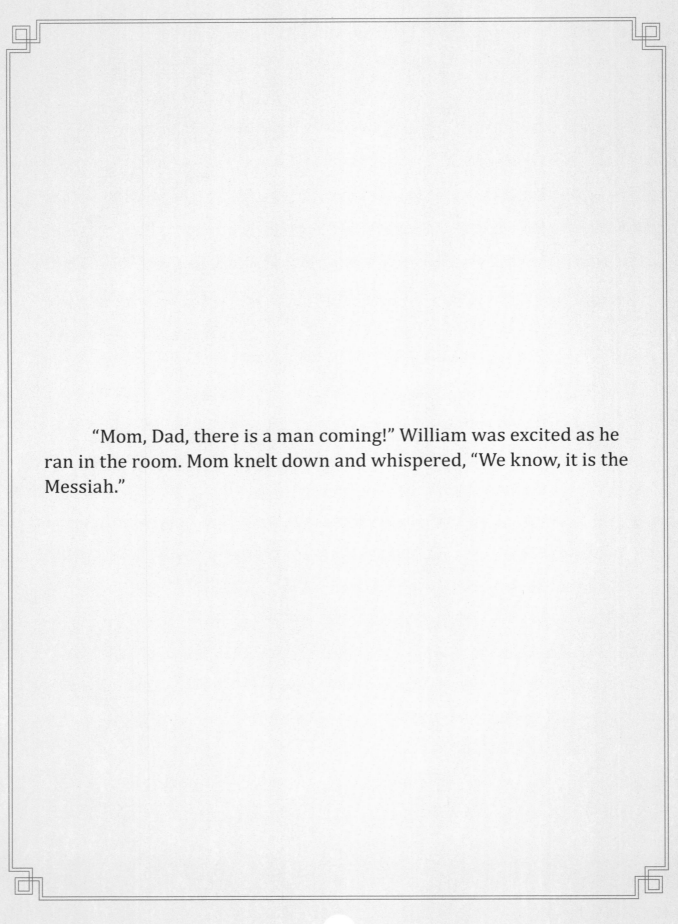

"Mom, Dad, there is a man coming!" William was excited as he ran in the room. Mom knelt down and whispered, "We know, it is the Messiah."

"The Messiah?" William asked.

"Yes, Jesus of Nazareth. Remember He is the one that heals the sick and fed the thousands with only five loaves and two little fish," Mom explained.

They left their little house and made their way down the street. A man came up beside them and said, "Jesus is just outside of town on the mountainside. Just look for the crowd, hurry!"

"Is he a prophet?" William asked.

"He is more than that. He is the Son of God," Dad said as excitement filled his face.

"Let's hurry. I want to see Him. Let's go!" William was ready.

As they made their way outside of town, William was amazed at the people who were coming out to see this man called Jesus.

As they walked a little farther, William saw many people. Many of them were sick, blind, and lame. All were hoping to be touched by Jesus and be healed.

As they topped a little hill, the family could see a large crowd in the small valley below.

Dad pointed with his finger and said, "There is Jesus on the other side. There He is!" The family moved closer.

When they came upon the crowd, everyone was silent so they could hear every word that Jesus said.

William grasped hold of his mom's hand, pulling her to him as he whispered, "I want to see Jesus. Let's go a little closer, please."

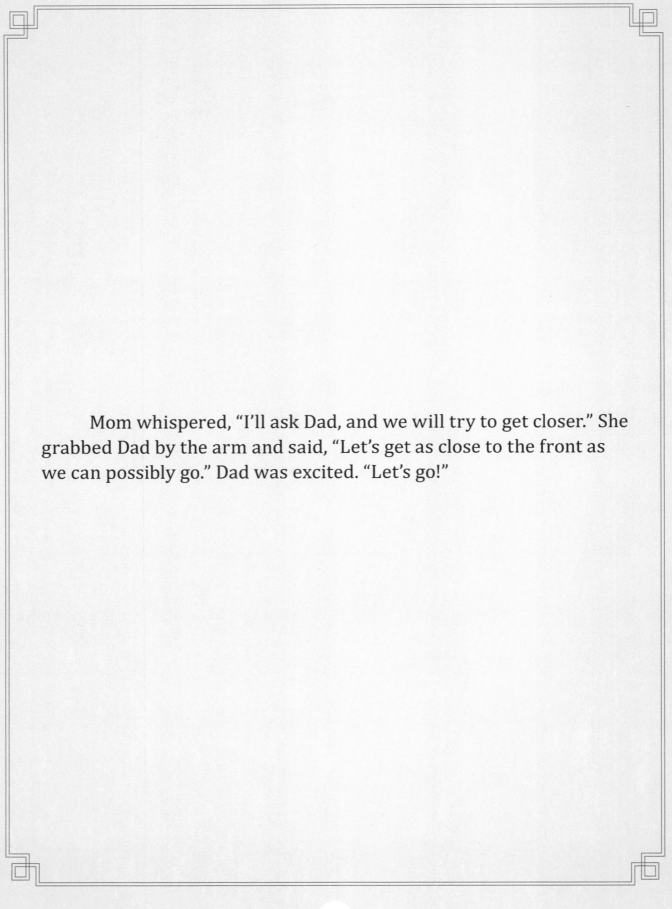

Mom whispered, "I'll ask Dad, and we will try to get closer." She grabbed Dad by the arm and said, "Let's get as close to the front as we can possibly go." Dad was excited. "Let's go!"

Slowly, they moved through the crowd. Inch by inch, yard by yard, until the family was seated at Jesus's feet.

Jesus spoke about marriage and to love your wife or husband. William said to himself, "Wow! Mom and Dad love each other already."

When Jesus ended his speech, someone stood up and said, "Bring the children to Jesus so He can touch and bless them."

Jesus said, "Bring the little ones to Me."

William ran as fast as he could go. He was the first to reach Jesus. William hugged Him and said, "I love you, Jesus."

Jesus looked down at William. "I love you too. You and your family are very blessed."

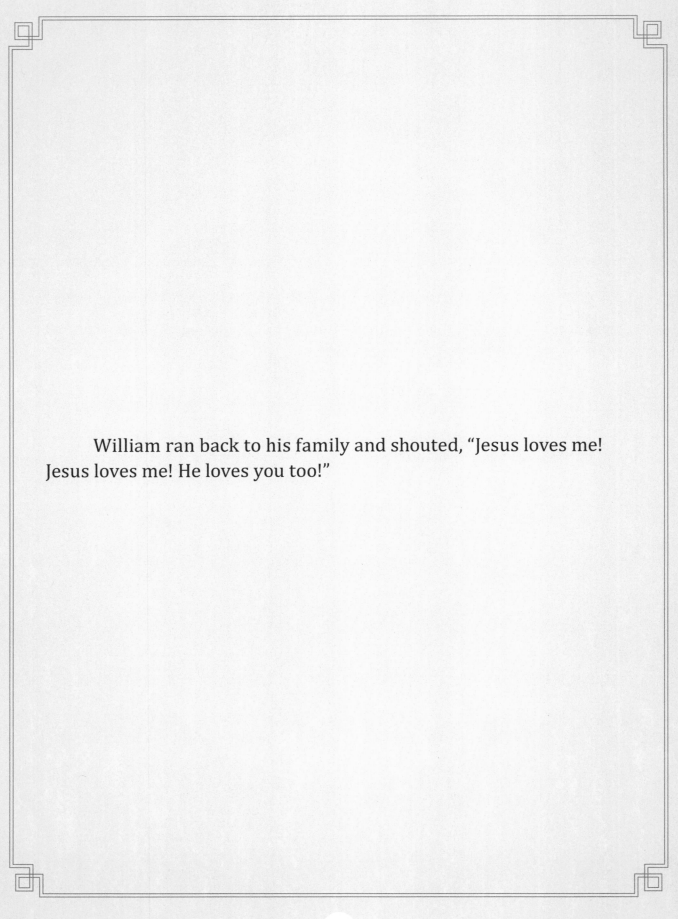

William ran back to his family and shouted, "Jesus loves me! Jesus loves me! He loves you too!"

Printed in the United States
by Baker & Taylor Publisher Services